MW01518984

The Truth Unveiled

(Kashf-ul-Ghita)

Hazrat Mirza Ghulam Ahmad

The Promised Messiah and Mahdi[as],
Founder of the Ahmadiyya Muslim Community

ISLAM INTERNATIONAL PUBLICATIONS LTD.

The Truth Unveiled
English translation of *Kashf-ul-Ghita*

Written by Hazrat Mirza Ghulam Ahmad
The Promised Messiah and Mahdi, peace be upon him,
Founder of the Ahmadiyya Muslim Community

First published in Urdu in Qadian, India 1898
Present English translation published in the UK 2016

© Islam International Publications Ltd.

Published by
Islam International Publications Ltd.
Islamabad, Sheephatch Lane
Tilford, Surrey GU10 2AQ
United Kingdom

Printed and bound by
CPI Group (UK) Ltd.
Croydon, CR0 4YY

For more information please visit www.alislam.org.

ISBN 978-1-84880-083-0

CONTENTS

Hazrat Mirza Ghulam Ahmad of Qadian
The Promised Messiah & Mahdi
(peace be upon him)

ABOUT THE AUTHOR

Hazrat Mirza Ghulam Ahmad, peace be upon him, was born in 1835 in Qadian, India. From his early life, he dedicated himself to prayer, the study of the Holy Quran and other scriptures. He was deeply pained to observe the plight of Islam, which was being attacked from all directions. In order to defend Islam and present its teachings in their pristine purity, he wrote more than ninety books, thousands of letters and participated in many religious debates. He argued that Islam is a living faith, which can lead humanity to the achievement of moral and spiritual perfection by establishing communion with God.

Hazrat Mirza Ghulam Ahmad, peace be upon him, started experiencing divine dreams, visions and revelations at a young age. In 1889, under divine command, he started accepting initiation into the Ahmadiyya Muslim Community. He continued to receive divine revelations and was thereafter commanded by God to announce that he was the divinely appointed Reformer of the Latter Days, as prophesied by various religions under different titles. He claimed to be the same Promised Messiah and Mahdi whose advent had been prophesied by the Holy Prophet Muhammad, peace and blessings of Allah be upon him. The

Ahmadiyya Muslim Community is now established in more than two hundred countries of the world.

After the demise of the Promised Messiah, peace be upon him, the institution of *Khilafat* (successorship) was established in 1908 to continue his mission, in fulfilment of the prophecies made in the Holy Quran and by the Holy Prophet Muhammad, peace and blessings of Allah be upon him. Hazrat Mirza Masroor Ahmad, may Allah be his Helper, is the Fifth Successor to the Promised Messiah, peace be upon him, and the present head of the Ahmadiyya Muslim Community.

PUBLISHER'S NOTE

The words in the text in normal brackets () and in between the long dashes—are the words of the Promised Messiah, peace be upon him, and if any explanatory words or phrases are added by the translator for the purpose of clarification, they are put in square brackets [ ].

References to the Holy Quran contain the name of the *Surah* [i.e. chapter] followed by a chapter:verse citation, e.g. *Surah Al-Jumu'ah*, 62:4, and counts *Bismillahir-Rahmanir-Rahim* [In the name of Allah, the Gracious, the Merciful] as the first verse in every chapter it appears.

The name of Muhammad[sa], the Holy Prophet of Islam, has been followed by the symbol [sa], which is an abbreviation for the salutation *Sallallahu Alayhi Wa Sallam* (peace and blessings of Allah be upon him). The names of other Prophets and Messengers are followed by the symbol [as], an abbreviation for *Alayhis-Salam* (peace be upon him). The actual salutations have not generally been set out in full, but they should nevertheless, be understood as being repeated in full in each case.

Publisher

اے قادرِخدا

اس گورنمنٹ عالیہ انگلشیہ کو ہماری طرف سے نیک جزا دے

اور اُس سے نیکی کر جیسا کہ اُس نے ہم سے نیکی کی ۔ آمین

كشفُ الغطاء

یعنی

ایک اسلامی فرقہ کے پیشوا مرزا غلام احمد قادیانی کی طرف سے بحضور گورنمنٹ
عالیہ اُس فرقہ کے حالات اور خیالات کے بارے میں اطلاع اور نیز اپنے خاندان
کا پکھ ذکر اور اپنے مشن کے اصولوں اور ہدایتوں اور تعلیموں کا بیان اور نیز
اُن لوگوں کی خلاف واقعہ باتوں کا ردّ جو اس فرقہ کی نسبت غلط خیالات
پھیلانا چاہتے ہیں ۔

اور یہ مؤلف

تاجِ عزت جناب ملکہ معظمہ قیصرِ ہند دام اقبالہا کا واسطہ ٹُ الکر
بخدمت گورنمنٹ عالیہ انگلشیہ کے اعلیٰ افسروں اور معزز حکام کی باب
گذارش کرتا ہے کہ براہِ غریب پروری و کرم گستری اس رسالہ کو اوّل سے
آخر تک پڑھا جائے یا ئن لیا جائے

یہ رسالہ تالیف ہوکر مورخہ ۲۰ سپتمبر سنہ ۱۸۹۸ء بمقام قادیان ضلع گورداسپور میں پنجاب چشمۂ نور ضیاء الاسلام مطبع جناب میر عباس حسین صاحب سلمہ علی میں چھپا ہوا

تعداد ۳۵۰۰

O Almighty God!
We pray that You may grant a good reward to the
eminent British government and be benevolent to it
as it has been benevolent to us. Ameen.

THE TRUTH UNVEILED

viz.

A treatise presented to the esteemed government by **Mirza Ghulam Ahmad** of Qadian, the spiritual leader of a denomination in Islam, to enunciate the circumstances and ideologies of his sect and to give a brief account of his family history; and further, to elaborate on the principles, precepts and teachings of his mission and to counter the false accusations levelled by those who desire to disseminate falsehood regarding this sect.

The author respectfully requests the eminent officials and honourable ministers of the British government that, for the sake of Her Majesty the Empress of India, may her prosperity endure, they may, as a favour to my humble self, read this treatise of mine or hear it from beginning to end.

PRINTED 27 DECEMBER 1898 AT ZIYA-UL-ISLAM PRESS, QADIAN, UNDER THE AUSPICES OF ITS PROPRIETOR, HAKEEM FAZL-UD-DEEN

Copies: 350

Translation of the original Urdu title page for *Kashf-ul-Ghita*.

I request the revered officers to read this treatise carefully from beginning to end for the sake of Her Majesty the Empress of India, may her prosperity endure.

بِسْمِ اللّٰهِ الرَّحْمٰنِ الرَّحِيْمِ [1]

نَحْمَدُهٗ وَنُصَلِّيْ عَلٰى رَسُوْلِهِ الْكَرِيْمِ [2]

I, Ghulam Ahmad, son of Mirza Ghulam Murtaza, am a resident of Qadian, District Gurdaspur, Punjab and the leader of a well renowned sect that can be found in many areas of the Punjab. Moreover, the members of my community also reside in many districts of India including Hyderabad, Bombay, and Madras; the Arabian Peninsula, Syria, and Bukhara. Thus, I have thought it prudent to pen this brief treatise so that the senior officials of this **benevolent government** might come to know of my circumstances and the views of my community. For I witness that this new sect continues to progress day by day in these countries; many Indian officials, respectable nobles, landlords, and celebrated merchants have entered the fold and continue to do so. As a result, deep-rooted animosity and malice has arisen against me amongst ordinary Muslims and their clerics. It is possible that their envy might incite them to make misleading representations to the government. Therefore, through this treatise, I intend to convey my

---

1. In the name of Allah, the Gracious, the Merciful. [Publisher]
2. We praise Him and invoke blessings upon His Noble Messenger[sa]. [Publisher]

actual circumstances and the principles of my mission to this kind government.

For the purpose of clarity, I have divided the exposition of these matters into five sections.

Firstly, I shall comment upon my lineage and background. In this context, it should suffice to say that I belong to a landowning family. My ancestors were sovereigns in the land and independent ruling chieftains who were ruined unexpectedly during the Sikh rule. Although the favours of the British government have bene-fited all in general, still, my elders in particular are most indebted as under British protection they were delivered from a raging fur-nace and granted peace after a life of peril.

My father, Mirza Ghulam Murtaza, was a chieftain in this locality known for his piety. The eminent governmental officials have given strong written testimonial to his faithfulness and **loy-alty** to the government. He was always honoured with a seat when in audience with the governor; senior officials would always look toward him with respect. Due to his noble character, both pro-vincial and divisional officers would, on occasions, visit him at his home, for in the eyes of British officials he was a loyal chieftain. I firmly believe that the British government will never forget the service he rendered during the perilous time of **1857** when, beyond the measure of his means, he himself purchased **fifty horses** and gifted them to the government as support along with the service of **fifty horsemen** from among his family and friends. Numerous riders from among our relations bravely lost their lives in India against the mutineers. My brother, the late Mirza Ghulam Qadir, participated in the battle of **Trimmu** Ghat and fought valiantly. Thus, my ancestors have sacrificed their blood, wealth and lives;

and by their continuous services, have proved their loyalty to the government. I am convinced that on account of these very services, the eminent government shall not count our family merely amongst its general subjects, nor forget our rightful claims which stem from our role during the Great Rebellion.[1] In his book, *The Panjab* [sic] *Chiefs*, Sir Lepel Griffin has also mentioned my father and brother Mirza Ghulam Qadir. Below, I have reproduced several letters from senior officials in which the services of my revered father and brother are briefly discussed.

---

1. This refers to the 1857 Indian mutiny, also known as the 'Great Rebellion'. [Publisher]

Translation of Certificate
of J. M. Wilson.

To

Mirza Ghulam Murtaza
khan Chief of Qadian.

I have perused your
application reminding me
of your and your family's
past services and rights I
am well aware that since
the introduction of the British
Gov't you & your family have
certainly remained devoted
faithful & steady subjects
& that your rights are really
worthy of regard. In every
respect you may rest assured
and satisfied that the British
Gov't will never forget your
family's rights & services
which will receive due con-
-sideration when a favorable
opportunity offers itself.

you must continue to
faithful and devoted subjects
in it lies the satisfaction of the
Gov't and your welfare.

11–6–1849 Lahore

Facsimile of the original page printed in 1898.

Translation of Certificate of J. M. Wilson

To
    Mirza Ghulam Murtaza Khan Chief of Qadian.

I have perused your application reminding me of your and your family's past services and rights. I am well aware that since the introduction of the British Govt. you & your family have certainly remained devoted faithful & steady subjects & that your rights are really worthy of regard. In every respect you may rest assured and satisfied that the British Govt. will never forget your family's rights & services which will receive due consideration when a favorable opportunity offers itself.

    You must continue to be faithful and devoted subjects as in it lies the satisfaction of the Govt. and your welfare.

11-6-1849 Lahore

Transcript of the original page.

Translation of Mr Robert Cust's Certificate

To

Mirza Ghulam Murtaza Khan chief of Qadian

As you rendered great help in enlisting sowars & supplying horses to Govt in the mutiny of 1857 and maintained loyalty since its beginning up to date and thereby gained the favor of Govt a <u>khilat</u> worth Rs 200/- is presented to you in recognition of good services and as a reward for your loyalty.

Moreover in accordance with the wishes of chief Commissioner as conveyed in his no 576 dy 10th August 58 this parwana is addressed to you as a token of satisfaction of Govt for your fidelity and repute.

Facsimile of the original page printed in 1898.

Translation of Mr. Robert Cast's Certificate

To

Mirza Ghulam Murtaza Khan Chief of Qadian

As you rendered great help in enlisting sowars & supplying horses to Govt. in the mutiny of 1857 and maintained loyalty since its beginning up to date and thereby gained the favor of Govt, a <u>khilat</u> worth Rs.200/ is presented to you in recognition of good services and as a reward for your loyalty.

Moreover in accordance with the wishes of chief Commissioner as conveyed in his no. 576 d/ 10th August 58 this parwana is addressed to you as a token of satisfaction of Govt. for your fidelity and repute.

Transcript of the original page.

Translation of sir Robert Egerton
Financial Commr's murasala dy 29
June 1876

My dear friend Ghulam Qadir.

I have perused your letter of the 2nd
instant & deeply regret the death of your
father Mirza Ghulam Murtaza who was
a great well wisher and faithful chief
of Govt.

In consideration of your family services
I will esteem you with the same respects
as that bestowed on your loyal father.
I will keep in mind the restoration
and welfare of your family when a
favorable opportunity occurs.

Facsimile of the original page printed in 1898.

Translation of Sir Robert Egerton
Financial Commr's Mursala d/ 29, June 1876

My dear friend Ghulam Qadir,

I have perused your letter of the 2nd instant & deeply regret the death of your father Mirza Ghulam Murtaza who was a great well wisher and faithful chief of Govt.

In consideration of your family services, I will esteem you with the same respect as that bestowed on your loyal father. I will keep in mind the restoration and welfare of your family when a favorable opportunity occurs.

Transcript of the original page.

Such were the circumstances of my father and brother. But, since I have passed an austere and ascetic life, it is in my own humble way that I have engaged in assisting and supporting the British government. For nineteen years or thereabouts, I have spent time publishing books in which it is mentioned that the Muslims ought to serve the government with heartfelt sincerity and should demonstrate greater loyalty and devotion than other peoples. It was for this purpose that I wrote certain books in Arabic and others in Persian, and disseminated them in faraway countries. In every one of these publications, through logical reasoning, I repeatedly urged and persuaded the Muslims to show obedience to the state with heart and soul. These books have been distributed as far as the Arab Peninsula, Syria, Kabul, and Bukhara. However, I have been informed that after reading them, certain ignorant clerics from among the Muslims have declared that I am a disbeliever. They consider my writings to stem from a secret and confidential alliance between myself and the British Empire, and they believe that I am remunerated by the government for this.

However, I have come to know for certain that the hearts of some learned people have been positively influenced by my writings and they have repented from the barbaric doctrines, which were leading them to act in contradiction to the objectives of the government. My writings on religious matters in opposition to the Christian priests have yielded very powerful results in creating this positive attitude. In addition, I have strongly invited the Muslims to obey the government and have admonished the ignorant mullahs of the Frontier Region, who constantly create disturbances and incite the Afghans to rise in rebellion. These vigorous writings in support of the British government would have been intolerable to the biased and ignorant Muslims. However, when erudite persons find in my writings expositions in support of Islam on the one hand and hear my admonishments exhorting them to show sincere faithfulness and obedience to the government on the other, they cannot view me with mistrust. How can they? Indeed, Muslims have been commanded by God and His Messenger to faithfully obey the government they live under. I have fully elaborated upon these religious injunctions in my books. Thus, the government can conclude that just as my father was truly loyal to the government and my brother also followed in his footsteps, I too have rendered such service through my pen for the last nineteen years. How, then, can my affairs be suspicious? My entire youth was spent in this way. Now, I approach old age and find myself constantly ill. I am approximately sixty years of age. A person who declares me to be a threat to the government is severely unjust.

I cannot deny that I have also authored books on religious matters, nor do I deny that writings authored by me, which stand in opposition to the dogmas of the Christian clergy have been published as well, and they are dissatisfied by this due to their religious persuasions. But, I consider my good intentions, of which God Almighty is fully aware, to be sufficient. The way I show my opposition is completely at variance with the behaviour of other Muslims. It is not my view in the least that religious differences should cause such anger that the response of the opposition be legislated by the government as a crime punishable by law, or that enmity be harboured against such people. On the contrary, my philosophy is that patience and propriety ought to be demonstrated in religious debates. It is for this reason that when other Muslims sent memorials to the government through the Anjuman-i-Himayat-i-Islam to have the author of *Ummahat-ul-Mu'minin*[1] prosecuted, I opposed them and on the contrary, dispatched a memorial stating clearly that Islam teaches forbearance and forgiveness whenever feelings are hurt in religious matters.

The Quran explicitly teaches us that during a religious discourse, if one's sentiments are injured by offensive language, such a person ought not to behave like those who are narrow-minded and approach the courts. Rather, one ought to show patience and good grace. The Quran clearly teaches us to show love, good conduct, and virtue to the Christians. However, that is not to say that there is anything amiss with a religious debate that is undertaken with good intentions and sympathy, in order to disseminate the truth and create a spirit of peace and harmony.

The second section relates to the teachings of my mission. I have been publishing my teaching for approximately nineteen years. Moreover, by way of summary, I have published my teachings in announcements printed on 29 May 1898 and 27 February 1895, and all of these books and announcements have been published and have gained wide publicity in the Punjab and throughout India. My teaching, in summary, is nothing more than this: Believe that God is One and without partner; be kind to God's servants; be virtuous in your deeds and intentions; be such that

---

1. *Ummahat-ul-Mu'minin* or literally, *Mothers of the Faithful,* was an extremely hurtful and profane book published by a Christian in which vicious attacks were made against the Holy Prophet[sa] and his noble wives. [Publisher]

no evil or mischief dare approach your hearts; do not tell lies or slander; do not harm another person through your words or actions; eschew all forms of sin; control your inner desires; seek to become pure-hearted and noble; show true loyalty and obedience to the British government under whose protection your wealth, honour, and life are safe; let compassion towards all people be the guiding principle of your life; safeguard your hands, tongues, and your inner thoughts from every kind of evil scheme, mischievous conspiracy, and treachery; fear God and worship Him with pure-heartedness; do not yield to injustice, iniquity, misappropriation, bribery, violation of rights, or prejudice; avoid bad company and the trespassing of the eyes; protect the ears from listening to back-biting; do not seek to harm or injure anyone, irrespective of their religion, nation, or people; become a good counsellor to everyone; do not sit in the company of those who cause unrest and who are evil, indecent, and immoral; safeguard against every sin and seek to perform every good deed; your hearts ought to be free from deceit; your hands ought not to be responsible for injustice; your eyes ought to be free from impurity; you should never conspire to bring about any evil or rebellion; fervently seek to recognise God, meeting whom is true deliverance and finding whom is true salvation.

God reveals Himself only to those who search for Him with love and sincerity of heart. He manifests Himself unto those who become His alone. Pure hearts are the throne upon which He settles. Tongues which are untainted by falsehood, abuse, and absurdities are the abode of His revelation. And those who immerse themselves in His pleasure become a manifestation of His miraculous power.

This is an illustration of the teachings which have been imparted to this community for nineteen years. Therefore, I am certain that this community is God-fearing and sincerely obedient. They are grateful to the British government and well-wishers of all humanity. They are not consumed by barbaric passions and beastly characteristics. If the senior officials of the government would take the least bit of trouble and closely read my publications of the past nineteen years, they would find that the teachings I have outlined above, by way of illustration, are found in the majority of my books.

No one can remain the follower of another unless he finds a complete consistency between the words and deeds of their master. So if my actions were contradictory to the words that I have expressed above by way of illustration, how could an intelligent person continue to have faith in me, inasmuch as a large part of my community consists of intelligent and educated people? Some of them hold respectable positions in the government such as revenue officers and extra assistants. There are lawyers, doctors, assistant surgeons, wealthy nobles, chieftains and merchants of the Punjab as well. From time to time I have been publishing their names. Any wise person can understand that there is nothing more unethical than to teach one thing but to act differently in secret. Is it possible for good-hearted and wise persons to share company with such an evil individual for even a moment?

It will bring great satisfaction to the government to learn that the people of my community are not ignorant, barbaric, wicked, immoral, or ill-mannered. In fact, they are so renowned in their virtue and righteousness that even in the eyes of the government, many of them are known to be pious, good-tempered, pure-hearted and loyal citizens. Some have even been conferred respectable posts by the government. In his last few days, just prior to his demise, **Sir Syed Ahmad Khan** KCSI published a testimony about me. From this the noble government can conclude that this wise and perceptive individual held my conduct and character in very high regard. I present his words in the footnote below.☆

☆   *Mirza Ghulam Ahmad of Qadian*

In his announcement of 25 June 1897, Mirza Sahib has written an excellent sentence regarding loyalty and allegiance to the British government. In my opinion, all Muslim subjects of the British government ought to be as Mirza Sahib writes; therefore, I hereby publish Mirza Sahib's words in my newspaper. Mirza Sahib writes:

    The critique made against me for showing loyalty to the British government stems from sheer mischief. The facts pertaining to the Sultan of Rome are a separate issue, but our obligations to this government are nonetheless well established, for to show ingratitude is a kind of faithlessness.
    O ignorant people! My praise for the British government does not flow from my pen by way of hypocrisy, as does yours. Rather, it is my faith and belief that in truth, by the grace of God Almighty, His sanctuary is given to us through this government. In my view, what greater evidence can there be of the peaceful rule of this government than the fact that it is under this administration that God Almighty has chosen to establish this righteous community. I consider those persons wretched traitors who flatter and fall before the British officials in their presence and then, when they return to their homes, aver that whosoever is thankful to this administration is a disbeliever. Know well that my behaviour towards this government is not hypocritical *وَلَعْنَةُ اللّٰهِ عَلَى الْمُنَافِقِيْنَ. This is the very belief that rests in my heart.*
              (Aligarh Institute Gazette and Tahzibul Akhlaq, 24 July 1897)

I published this article on loyalty to the British government in the days when Maulvi Muhammad Husain of Batala and others published articles in praise of the Sultan of Rome. Because of my faithfulness to this

To summarise, my teaching is exactly as I have stated here by way of illustration. My community is a group of such respectable, modest and virtuous individuals that I can never even conceive that the government would deem them a threat, or suspicious in terms of behaviour and conduct. It is the good fortune of my community that no uncivilised, ignorant, and ill-mannered persons have been drawn towards me. Instead, my community is full of decent, esteemed and educated persons; Indian officials as well as civil servants working in respectable posts. Prejudiced and ignorant Muslims who are narrow-minded, and who are overpowered by barbaric and carnal passions, being short-sighted, have nothing to do with this community. Rather, they look upon it with enmity and hatred; they are engaged in scheming to wound our sentiments and go on proclaiming that we are heretics.

The third section relates to my affairs and it is imperative that I convey this to the government, as it has to do with the claims that I have made regarding religion on the basis of revelation. In this connection, certain miscreant and self-interested parties have presented these claims maliciously in their newspapers and magazines; they have made false statements and have relied on fabrications. I trust that there is not much need in the way of a reasoned discourse to convince my enlightened government that since time immemorial, it has been the law of nature that in order to increase

---

government, I was declared a heretic. Syed Ahmad Khan knew very well that I am an ardent well-wisher of the British government and a peace-loving individual. That is why I included the name of Syed Sahib as a witness in my favour during the lawsuit of Dr Clark. —Author

* And may the curse of Allah be upon the hypocrites. [Publisher]

the divine cognition of those who have been heedless, God, who is the Creator of this world and who gives everlasting hope and glad tidings of the life to come, confers revelation upon some of His servants and speaks with them, manifesting to them His heavenly signs. They begin to see Him with spiritual eyes and are filled with certainty and love to the extent that they become worthy enough to also draw others into the life-giving spring from which they drink so that those who have been heedless might also love God and attain everlasting salvation. Whenever the love of God begins to disappear from the world and true inner virtue begins to languish because of heedlessness, God confers His revelation upon one of His servants and raises him to cleanse the hearts. So in the present age it is my humble self whom God has purified by His own hand and raised for this task. It is my humble self who has been raised to sow the seed of true righteousness in the hearts of people, in the same way that a pure and holy man of God was raised about nineteen hundred years ago in the settlements of Galilee, during the era of the Roman Empire, to show the path to true salvation. During the administration of Pilate, he suffered greatly at the hands of the Jews and consequently was forced to migrate from those lands in accordance with the eternal practice of God. Thereafter, he came to India in order to convey the message of God Almighty to those Jews who had settled in these lands during the diaspora. Finally, at the age of 120, he bade farewell to this temporal abode and returned to his True Beloved, granting the land of Kashmir an eternal honour through his holy shrine.

How blessed are Srinagar, Anmuzah and the locality of Khanyar in that this eternal prince and pious Prophet of God left behind his pure remains in their blessed soil and granted many of

Kashmir's inhabitants eternal life and true salvation. Let the glory of God accompany him forever. *Ameen.* As this Prophet Prince came to the world in a state of modesty and humility—setting an example for the world in modesty, humility and forbearance— God has willed to raise **me** in the present age among those who are bereft of heavenly morals in the likeness of this Prophet Prince of Allah; I too hail from a noble and ruling family, and my apparent circumstances also closely resemble his. Thus, on account of this, God willed that I, too, live a modest and simple life in the world.

Since the earliest of days, divine scriptures had promised the appearance of such a person in the world; hence, God has named me the Promised Messiah—meaning a person who is similar to Jesus the Messiah in his morals. God raised the Messiah, peace be upon him, within the Roman Empire and the state did not bring him any deliberate harm. Instead, it was his fellow Jews who committed grave injustice against him, terribly insulted him and sought to present him as a traitor to the state. But I know that our empire, the British Empire—may God protect it—is far more transparent than the Romans with regards to its judicial system and the hearts of its officials are far greater than Pilate's in their intelligence, insight, and justice. The justice of this empire shines brighter than that of the Romans. Thus, gratitude is due for the grace of God Almighty that He has provided me the shade of the protection of such a government, which relies on investigation rather than conjecture.

Thus, the name 'Promised Messiah'—which has been chosen for me by the heavens—means only that in all moral aspects, the All-Sustaining God has made me the resemblance of the

Messiah, peace be upon him, so that through peace and kindness I may grant spiritual life to the people. I have not defined the title 'Promised Messiah' in this manner only today, rather, I did so in exactly the same way as far back as nineteen years ago in my book *Barahin-e-Ahmadiyyah*.

It is possible that many people might ridicule what I have to say, or denounce me as a fool or one deranged, as such matters are beyond the comprehension of the world. The world cannot understand them, particularly those Muslims who belong to some of the earlier sects and hold dangerous views about such prophecies. It is worth bearing in mind that the earlier sects among the Muslims await the arrival of a Mahdi who would be a descendant of Fatimah, the mother of Husayn. They also await a Messiah who will join forces with this Mahdi and wage war against the opponents of Islam. I, however, have insisted that all such notions are vain, false and fabricated. Those who adhere to them are in grave error.

The concept of such a Mahdi that has gripped the hearts of Muslims due to ignorance and deception, is fictitious. The truth is that no Mahdi will appear from among the children of Fatimah. All the Hadith that suggest this concept are fabricated, inauthentic, and forged, and were probably produced during the Abbasid dynasty. The only authentic and truthful narration is that a person bearing the name of Jesus, peace be upon him, will be raised, who will neither wage war, nor shed blood. Instead, he will turn the hearts of the people to the truth with modesty, humility, forbearance and reassuring signs. Accordingly, God has informed me with lucid discourse and clear signs that I am that individual. He has revealed signs from the heavens to establish my truth, has disclosed to me secrets of the unseen and events of the future, and has conferred upon me insights of which the world is unaware. Furthermore, my belief that a violent Mahdi will not appear in the world is at variance with the belief of all other Muslims.

I have imparted this doctrine to my entire community and to hundreds of thousands of people. This goes against the hopes of the Muslims. Without a doubt, their beliefs had aroused savage passions and distanced them from civility and decency. One who reflects can understand that a person holding such ideas is dangerous. Therefore, God, who is Ever-Merciful and Compassionate, has thus laid the foundations of peace with my advent. He has washed away these foolish ideas from the hearts of my community just as a cloth is cleansed with soap. It is due to this very reason that other people harbour enmity against me.

Contrary to the expectations of the Jews, the Messiah, peace be upon him, did not appear as a king, nor did he wage wars with the people of other nations. Ultimately, the Jews began to persecute him and averred that he was not the one they awaited. Much of the same has occurred with me, but there are other differences as well. As such, one view held by my opponents is that as far as possible, one ought to view others with enmity and when the opportunity arises, cause them harm as well. But I say that no one can ever be a true Muslim until he has good feelings for others just as he does for himself. It is my exhortation that you ought to purify your hearts and show compassion to the whole of humanity, not wishing evil for anyone, for this is the height of morality.

It is regrettable that these people are eager to exact retribution on other nations, but I say that you should act with forgiveness and compassion and not with malice or hypocrisy. Show mercy in the earth so that the heavens show mercy to you.

These are not mere words; I have actually demonstrated this through my practice. I have never desired to injure an individual who seeks to cause me harm. For example, Dr Clark accused me of attempted murder but this could not be proven in a court of law. In fact, the evidence proved more detrimental to him. Afterwards, Captain Douglas, the Magistrate of District Gurdaspur, asked me if I would like to counter-sue Dr Clark, but I unreservedly declined. As a matter of fact, I even refrained from lodging a case against those Christians who, in accordance with the Court's investigation, were proven guilty of wrongdoing. If forgiveness and compassion were not my practice, then after bearing such anguish I would most certainly have pursued the matter further.

Similarly, when the Muslims of this area, acting through the Anjuman-i-Himayat-i-Islam Lahore, sought to have the author of the booklet *Ummahat-ul-Mu'minin* punished and sent numerous memorials to the Lieutenant Governor Bahadur to this effect, expressing their deep outrage, even at that time, I dispatched a memorial against this. I clearly wrote that I sought no retribution from the author of *Ummahat-ul-Mu'minin;* rather, I considered it my obligation to sensibly pen a rebuttal.

Thus, in matters such as these, there has always existed a difference of opinion between myself and these people along with their clergy. They are greatly aggravated by this, but for my part I harbour no enmity against them.✩ In any case, I believe that they are

---

✩ **Note:** Maulvi Muhammad Husain appeared as a witness for the prosecution in the case brought by Dr Clark. My lawyer, Maulvi Fazl Deen,

pitiable. Who is more pitiable than one who abandons the path of truth and rectitude?

One difference of belief between us relates to the death of the Messiah, peace be upon him, and this has greatly agitated my opponents. After thorough research, I have proven that the Messiah, peace be upon him, has passed away. I have found firm evidences that God Almighty saved him from the cross and sent him toward India to preach to the Jews who were forced to disperse by Nebuchadnezzar to Persia, Tibet, and Kashmir, and who then settled in these lands. As such, he remained in these lands for quite some time, imparting the message of Allah, and ultimately expired in Srinagar. His holy tomb is located in Mohalla Khanyar, Srinagar, known as the final resting place of the Prince **Prophet, Yuz Asaf.**☆ The name *Yasu*, like Jesus, has taken on the form Yuz Asaf due to linguistic variation.

The fourth section comprises an elaboration on how the Muslim scholars have reacted to me after my claims. The details

---

sought my permission to ask Muhammad Husain a question which would greatly disgrace him before the Court. However, I steadfastly refused. If I had enmity for anyone in the world, then why would I have acted in this manner? —Author

☆ There are certain esteemed Kashmiri communities who include the word 'Jew' as part of their name, for it is an age old symbol of their national identity, establishing them as being from the Children of Israel, as 'Jew' denotes Jewish people. In English the word 'Jew' is also used in the same sense. Apart from this manifest proof which relates to the similarity of names within nations, a renowned French traveller, Dr Bernier, has recorded compelling evidence and testimonies of illustrious scholars in one of his travelogues, to prove that the people of Kashmir are, in fact, the Children of Israel. —Author

are that after hearing my claim to be the Promised Messiah and coming to know that I reject their barbaric depictions of a Mahdi who would cause rivers of blood to flow in the earth, a person from among the clerics, by the name of Muhammad Husain, who is the editor of the periodical *Isha'at-us-Sunnah* and a resident of Batala, District Gurdaspur, issued an edict of disbelief against me and obtained the signatures of a number of other Muslim clerics. I was denounced as a heretic and an antichrist. This was to the extent that the edict stated that I was deserving of death; that it was lawful to usurp our wealth and to forcefully seize our women and marry them. All this was deemed proper; rather, it was considered a means of divine reward.☆ Both these edicts were recorded as such in an announcement issued on 29 Ramadan 1308 A.H. from the Haqqani Printing Press Ludhiana and on the back page of *Sayf-e-Maslul* published by Egerton Press Rawalpindi at the behest of Muhammad Husain.

However, when no one was able to act upon these edicts out of fear of the British government, Muhammad Husain contrived another plan,* which was to constantly injure my sentiments through extremely abusive invectives and hurtful words, as he has done so at various places in an 1898 issue of *Isha'at-us-Sunnah*.

☆ **Note:** In truth, Muhammad Husain of Batala believes in the future advent of a violent Mahdi but he only deceives the government by saying that he holds no such belief. Yet time and again his real beliefs have come to light. If the government were to gather the other Muslim clerics and ask them about his beliefs regarding the Mahdi, his misrepresentation to the government and the actual belief, which he expresses to his brethren, i.e. other scholars, would soon become apparent. —Author

* See *Isha'at-us-Sunnah,* no. 5, vol. 18, p. 146, 154–155. —Author

In order to continue this practice of spewing invectives and foul language, he elicited the services of a mischievous individual by the name of Muhammad Bakhsh Jafar Zatalli—a resident of Lahore—and prepared all sorts of foul announcements himself, and published them in the said person's name. However, it was Muhammad Husain who perpetrated all this in secret and he also informed people of his actions. Moreover, he continued to boast that this was his own doing in his magazines.

All these vile announcements, which Muhammad Husain has been publishing most mischievously for a year or a little more, are composed in a most unwholesome and filthy manner. Every conceivable attempt has been made to dishonour, disgrace, slander, and humiliate me in these announcements; they are full of such foul and vulgar accusations that I cannot imagine even the worst dregs of society adopting such shameless and brazen methods against their enemies. From among these announcements, one was published on 12 August 1898 by the Taj-ul-Hind Press. A second announcement was published on 25 September 1898, by the Fakhr-ud-Deen Press Lahore. Likewise, a third announcement and an addendum were published on 11 June 1897 by the same printing house. I shall record, for the authorities, certain excerpts from these four announcements, in order to show the extent to which they have sought to defame me. They have been publishing such filthy announcements for not a month or two, but an entire year. After suffering these multiple wounds,☆ I was forced to write an announcement of my own, which was issued on 21 November

---

☆ I did not publish the prayer-duel announcement of 21 November 1898 until the opposing party had made numerous requests to me for a

1898, in which I besought God Almighty to dishonour the one who lies.

All four announcements of Muhammad Husain, which were published under Jafar Zatalli's name, contain very harsh, foul, and vulgar language in order to dishonour me. For example, it is written about me: 'The wife of this individual has relations with some of his followers.' Then, he tauntingly declares himself to be a recipient of divine revelation and writes that it was revealed to him: 'The wife of this individual will marry Muhammad Bakhsh Jafar Zatalli.'

Further, heaping scorn on me, he writes that it was revealed to him: 'The Qadiani will become entangled in a fatal lawsuit and be incarcerated by the English with his feet tied in chains and forced into exile. During his captivity he will lose his mind and senses completely; he will be afflicted with fistula; struck by leprosy; his body will be fed on by numerous insects; his appearance will be disfigured beyond recognition; and his beloved wife will have relations with some of his followers and then wander aimlessly; she will divorce the Qadiani and she will marry Muhammad Bakhsh Jafar Zatalli, and Maulvi Abu Sa'eed Muhammad Husain will solemnize the marriage.☆ In the end the Qadiani will lose his sight, hearing, and power of speech, and after committing suicide,

---

prayer-duel. As such, apart from these announcements, Muhammad Husain has himself published a letter of Jafar Zatalli dated 19 November 1898 and five consecutive announcements challenging me to a prayer-duel. —Author

☆ With great ridicule, Maulvi Muhammad Husain has written in an 1898 issue of *Isha'at-us-Sunnah:* 'I will solemnize the marriage of his wife with Muhammad Bakhsh.' —Author

he will be hurled into the flames of Hell.' He then jeeringly writes
at the end: 'All these revelations have been fulfilled, only the marriage remains.' Then, in the third announcement he derisively
writes: 'I have heard that this person has been struck down by the
plague and dogs have devoured his flesh.' Then, in the issue of July
1897 he has drawn a caricature of me in the form of a **bear.**

Aside from this, in the 1898 issues of *Isha'at-us-Sunnah,*
Muhammad Husain has repeatedly alleged that I am ill-mannered,
malevolent towards the British government, and bloodthirsty.

So when the injustice perpetrated by Muhammad Husain and
his people, such as Muhammad Bakhsh Jafar Zatalli and others,
crossed all bounds and I was treated with such contempt that every
possible word of abuse was spewed out at me, and after numerous
challenges for a prayer-duel were sent to me, I finally published
an announcement on 21 November 1898, with the sole purpose
of beseeching God Almighty to humiliate whosoever between
us was a liar. Thereafter, I published a further clarification to this
announcement on 30 November 1898. Even after my announcement of 21 November 1898, Muhammad Husain sought to defame
me in countless places. He misrepresented my announcement of
21 November 1898 to make it seem as if I had threatened to murder him, despite the fact that I had thrice elucidated in this very
announcement that I merely sought the humiliation of whosoever
of the two of us was a liar.

When I came to know that Muhammad Husain was mis-
representing my announcement of 21st November, I published
an announcement on 30 November 1898 so that Muhammad
Husain would not go on misleading others by misrepresentation.

However, I have heard that even after this, he continued with his deception. If my two announcements of 21 November 1898 and 30 November 1898 were read by even a child of limited ability, he would unmistakably recognise that these announcements did not contain any prophecy regarding the murder of any individual. Instead, all they contain is a supplication for God to **humiliate** the one who is a liar and a revelation of mine in this context.☆ And it was for this reason that within my announcement of 21 November 1898, I also reproduced the announcement by Muhammad Husain, which was published in the name of Muhammad Bakhsh and Abul-Hasan of Tibet. My purpose in this was to show people that Muhammad Husain sought to humiliate me through his foul language and so I sought a verdict from God to disgrace, in the same manner, whomsoever of the two of us was a liar. I have appended English translations of my announcements of 21 November 1898 and 30 November 1898 at the end of this treatise.[1]

The question as to why I wrote this announcement of 21 November 1898 and whether there was any real need which

---

☆ The revelation *جَزَاءُ سَيِّئَةٍ بِمِثْلِهَا published in the announcement of 21 November 1898 shows that the one who is a liar will definitely be disgraced, but in the way that he sought to disgrace the other. So here the same type of disgrace he tried to inflict has been mentioned. —Author
* The recompense of evil is a penalty in proportion thereto. [Publisher]

1. We were unable to locate these announcements in the original manuscript. They are available in the original Urdu in *Majmu'a-e-Ishtiharat*, vol. 3, p. 57–62 and 67–73, published by *Ash-Shirkatul-Islamiyyah, Rabwah.* [Publisher]

justified me in doing so has just been answered; in that, for over a year I remained the target of abusive announcements. That is to say, for one year, Muhammad Husain and his cohorts continuously published vile announcements about me. In these announcements I was utterly denigrated and insulted; no stone was left unturned to abuse me, to the extent that, merely to cause mischief, my wife was accused of illicit relations and adultery. In the face of such offensive behaviour and disgrace, any individual would feel a sense of indignation and I was well within my rights to take the matter to court. But as one possessed of a humble and patient disposition, I did not take legal action. For about a year or so, Muhammad Husain and his cohorts continued to send me announcements in Qadian via post, which were replete with insulting language, even though I had never subscribed to these vile newspapers and announcements.

In short, I endured repeated injury of my sentiments through such abuse and slander for a significant period of time. Only thereafter did I publish an announcement on 21 November 1898 in good faith. This merely contained a supplication entreating God to humiliate the liar, but only in the way that he sought to humiliate the other.

The fifth section which I present here relates to what these people thought of me before I made these claims and the reason behind their animosity toward me now. It would be sufficient here to write that Sheikh Muhammad Husain of Batala, the editor of *Isha'at-us-Sunnah,* the chief of my opponents, was great in praising me before my claims. He considered me virtuous, saintly, the 'Pride of the Muslims' and truly loyal to the government.

As such, in the June/July/August 1884 issue of his magazine
Isha'at-us-Sunnah, he wrote about me on page 169:

This individual has proven himself so steadfast in the
service of Islam through his wealth, person, pen, tongue,
conduct and speech that seldom can a similar example be
found among the earlier Muslims.

On page 176 of the very same issue he writes:

I am acquainted with the circumstances and views of the
author of *Barahin-e-Ahmadiyyah* (i.e. myself) in a way
very few contemporaries are. Not only is the esteemed
writer my countryman, but from my earliest days he was
my class-fellow. His honourable father, Mirza Ghulam
Murtaza, proved through his actions to be loyal, devoted
and faithful to the government, by contributing fifty
horses in its support during the mutiny of 1857.

Again on pages 177-178 he writes:

In a humble way, Mirza Ghulam Ahmad has always been
engaged in supporting the British government. He has
repeatedly written that this government is a heavenly
blessing for the Muslims and the Merciful God has sent
this empire as a rain of mercy for them. To wage war and
undertake Jihad against such an empire is categorically
forbidden.

Similarly, Muhammad Husain has, in numerous other editions of *Isha'at-us-Sunnah,* given clear testimony about me that 'this individual is humble, forbearing and loyal to the British government.'

He stood by this testimony for many years and continued to do so until I rejected the deep-rooted beliefs of these people that a Mahdi would appear in the world who would wage war against the Christians and Jesus, peace be upon him, would descend from heaven to assist him, and no infidel would remain beyond their grips; the wealth of disbelievers would be given to the Muslim clerics as well as other Muslims so abundantly that they would be unable to tend to it.

I do not subscribe to such baseless and absurd myths. I have repeatedly written that these notions are not substantiated by the Hadith and Quran. They are entirely vain and fabricated. I have not only rejected them, but have also stated that I have come as the Promised Messiah in accordance with the will of God Almighty and with His revelation. I proclaim to the people that the current Muslim beliefs, which indicate that a Mahdi will be raised from among the Children of Fatimah and the Messiah will descend from the heavens to support him, and that both of them will wage war in the earth against the infidels and Christians, and great wealth will be accumulated to reward the Muslim clerics and their ilk are false and baseless notions. No one will come to wage such wars. On the contrary, the objective was only to spiritually reform the heedless and it is for this reformation that I have appeared. These people disliked my admonition because **the imaginary prospect of attaining millions of rupees** and plundering the wealth of others was lost to them completely, with the coming of a humble individual in the form of the Promised Messiah who forbids war, prohibits nefarious schemes of **sedition** and teaches a life of simplicity.

Thus, how could they ever be pleased with such a person? Consequently, they were compelled to issue edicts of death and crucifixion against this person. It was deemed an article of faith to take hold of and then forcefully marry my wife as well as other women of the community.☆ Moreover, to abuse and slander me and cast filthy aspersions upon my wife was deemed worthy of divine reward.

Then their fury and rage was invoked for a second time when Muhammad Husain generously praised the Sultan of Rome[1] in his magazine; whereas I, after meeting with a Roman ambassador, published an announcement stating that we owe greater loyalty and obedience to the British government than to the Sultan of Rome. We are far more indebted to this empire than to the Sultan. This written statement greatly incited the Muslim clerics and they hurled filthy abuse upon me. **Sir Syed Ahmad Khan** KCSI alone agreed with my position. I have recorded his words, which were published in his own newspaper, within the pages of this treatise. I say truthfully that aside from these reasons there are no other causes for their animosity against me. The esteemed officials of

---

☆ **Note:** See pages 34 and 40 of the book *Sayf-e-Maslul,* published by Egerton Press Rawalpindi (undated) and Maulvi Muhammad and company's announcement published by the Haqqani Press Ludhiana, 29 Ramadan 1308 A.H. —Author

1. In this passage the words 'Rome' and 'Roman' signify the Ottoman Empire. [Publisher]

the British government might ascertain the extent of their inhumanity by closely perusing their announcements.

The teaching which I have been imparting to my community for the last nineteen years is also not hidden from this benign government. I have made it incumbent upon my community not to respond to the evil of these people and to live a humble life and I too have made it obligatory upon myself to remain silent in the face of these vile allegations and slander. That is why my community and I have always remained silent in the face of such lewd remarks. Any fair-minded person could discern how hurtful the action of Maulvi Muhammad Husain was in his instigating one of his cohorts, Muhammad Bakhsh Jafar Zatalli, to publish an announcement about me alleging that my wife had illicit relations with the members of my community. However, I remained silent upon hearing this allegation. Then, in another announcement he wrote that he had come to know that I had died and my flesh had been devoured by dogs. But again, I showed forbearance. Then, he wrote that he received a revelation to the effect that my wife would stray and marry Muhammad Bakhsh Jafar Zatalli, with Muhammad Husain solemnising the marriage. But I still remained patient. In another announcement he declared and depicted me as a bear with a rope drawn around its neck along with a highly abusive caption. In yet another announcement he stated that it was revealed to him that I would be imprisoned and struck with leprosy. The same Muhammad Husain wrote in *Isha'at-us-Sunnah* that I was a murderer, a philanderer, and a rebel. After all of these announcements these people repeatedly invited me to take up a prayer-duel and even these challenges were made in vulgar language. Finally, I issued a gentle and kind announcement on 21 November 1898 and its only purpose was for God to **humiliate** whosoever of us was a liar. However, the revelation contained in this announcement came with the condition that such a one would suffer the same humiliation as he sought for the other.

In short, everything that has occurred between them and I until now is exactly as I have just mentioned. I am in possession of all of Muhammad Husain's and Muhammad Bakhsh Jafar Zatalli's obscene announcements, the content of which has been summarised in this treatise. I present their dates and places of publication below:

Date of Announcement	Name of Press	Detail
11 June 1897	Taj-ul-Hind, Lahore Takiyah Sadhwan	The title of this announcement is 'Appendix of Newspaper—Jafar Zatalli.' It was written on the instigation of Sheikh Muhammad Husain of Batala, the editor of *Isha'at-us-Sunnah*. The aforementioned Sheikh has admitted this fact in his *Isha'at-us-Sunnah* and in the presence of many witnesses. Numerous filthy prophecies have been recorded in this announcement.
26 June 1897	"	This was also written under the encouragement of Sheikh Muhammad Husain.
23 June 1897	"	This was also written at the behest of Sheikh Muhammad Husain.

26 May 1897	//	This announcement also carried a threat against my life.
20 August 1897	//	This was also written at the behest of Muhammad Husain and is full of abusive language.
7 April 1897	//	On page 4 column 3 it is written that Mirza has died and his corpse has been placed in a museum.[1]
Isha'at-us-Sunnah, Muhammad Husain of Batala, from 1891 to 1898		In all these magazines that were published from 1891 to 1898, Maulvi Muhammad Husain has slandered me in every conceivable way, abused me, and even admitted that all the vile announcements by Muhammad Bakhsh Jafar Zatalli were written at his behest and instruction; he also greatly praised Muhammad Bakhsh.

Finally, a matter worthy of attention for the officials is that hundreds of honourable and upright individuals bear testimony to the purity of my life, as do many respectable officials who belong to my community and are deemed highly trustworthy in the eyes of the government. Furthermore, respectable chiefs and merchants can also testify to my virtuous and noble conduct. I do not come from a family which has ever fallen under the suspicion

---

1. Not only has Muhammad Husain accepted in his *Isha'at-us-Sunnah* that all this abuse was instigated and taught by himself, but a number of respectable persons are witness to this fact as well that Muhammad Husain would even provide the script of these announcements penned by his own hand. —Author

of the British government, nor can it be proven that I have ever committed a criminal offence. A majority of the members of my community consists of respectable officials, chieftains and noble academics who would not maintain a relationship as followers with a person of ill-conduct. There exists no personal animosity or financial disagreement between Muhammad Husain and I; we are merely separated by a theological difference. For almost a year, these people have made it their practice to spew invectives and publish vulgar announcements about me. It is for this reason that after many announcements were sent to me for almost a year, and after they continued to publish requests for a prayer-duel, my good intention, fear of God, and forbearance guided me to issue a prayer-duel, seeking a decision from God Almighty instead of resorting to abusive language. I did not invent this method of undertaking a prayer-duel of my own accord—it has existed since the earliest days of Islam as a Sunnah. It is an Islamic practice to leave the verdict to God Almighty by means of a prayer-duel when two parties are unable to settle an affair. However, I did not pen this announcement in order to prophesy the death or ruin of any individual. My announcement, in summary, calls on God Almighty to humiliate the one who is unjust in the same manner that he seeks to disgrace the other.

It is surely not my practice to prophesy the death of someone on my own. There were certain individuals about whom prophecies were made in the past such as Deputy Atham and Pundit Lekh Ram; however, these people themselves insisted and being adamant, even provided handwritten statements that a prophecy be made about them. In the case of Lekh Ram, aside from my prophecy, he also made a prophecy about me and published an

announcement that in the space of three years I would succumb
to cholera. Further, not only did he willingly circulate my prophecy among thousands of people, but also categorically stated in
an announcement that my prophecy was made with his consent.

It is obvious that an opponent like Lekh Ram would never
have refrained from pressing charges against me upon hearing
such a prophecy, had it displeased him. Hundreds of persons
are aware of the fact that he sojourned in Qadian for almost two
months to extract this prophecy from me. Then, after the prophecy, he remained alive for five whole years and did not complain
to anyone that this prophecy had been made against his will. In
the end, according to the will of God Almighty, he perished from
this world within the designated time frame of the prophecy. Even
at the time of his death he did not express any suspicion about me,
because in his heart he knew that I was not a wicked man or a
conspirer. Can one who speaks through the Holy Spirit resemble
one who is immoral and guilty of satanic and nefarious deception? One who speaks from God cannot be humiliated before the
people.

We are eternally thankful that we live in the shade of a kind,
just and wise government. If the Muslim clerics from among my
people seethe at me, and consider me a liar and a wrongdoer, I call
on this benign government to come to a decision between us by
adjudicating on a **prophecy of the unseen future,** which I will
make from God and disclose; it will not relate to the piety or sin-
fulness of any individual nor have an impact on any human being,
yet my truth or falsity will hinge upon it. If I am thus proven a

liar, I will be ready to submit to any punishment. But **who from among them would ever agree to such a judgment?**

It is to be pitied that Muhammad Husain is well aware that Lekh Ram adamantly insisted upon seeking a prophecy and stayed in Qadian for a considerable length of time for this purpose. Furthermore, Deputy Abdullah Atham was himself well aware of the state laws. If I had made the prophecy about him without being prompted it is not possible that someone who was previously employed as an Extra Assistant would keep their own counsel. In the lawsuit with Dr Martyn Clark, I submitted a handwritten manuscript from him in which he demanded a prophecy. Moreover, the announcement relating to the prayer-duel that was published by me on 21 November 1898 did not specify any individual in particular; rather, it was only published to show the true face of the one who lies. However, it was only with caution and care, after I received repeated announcements and letters from Muhammad Husain and his companions that I published this announcement, and not before. I am in possession of all of these announcements asking for a prayer-duel. In short, the true account of all that transpired between the party of Muhammad Husain and I is exactly as I have just presented.

I have appended my announcements of 21 November 1898 and 30 November 1898 to the end of this treatise for the perusal of the officials.[1]

---

1. For some reason, these announcements were not included herewith. They are available in the *Majmua-e-Ishtiharat,* vol. 3, p. 57–62 and 67–73, published by *Ash-Shirkatul-Islamiyyah,* Rabwah. [Publisher]

In conclusion, I consider it an obligation to inform this wise and benign government that the clerics from among my people oppose me only because the teaching I impart to my community contradicts their yearnings and desires. I oppose the sort of beliefs they hold regarding their much awaited Mahdi and Messiah. God Almighty has made clear to me the inaccuracy and falsity of all the notions which indicate that such a Mahdi or Messiah would come into the world and shed blood in order to spread faith and religion. God has never willed the spread of religion in this manner.

If, in the time of our Messenger, peace and blessings of Allah be upon him, war was ever waged against the opponents, these wars were never meant to propagate religion; rather, they were merely defensive. That is to say, they only took place because the opponents of that time, on account of their ignorant religious prejudice, desired to eradicate the Muslims from the face of the earth. They would slaughter the Muslims, inflict great suffering upon them and prevent them from freely conveying the message of Islam. Hence, these opponents who unjustly slaughtered innocent Muslims merely due to religious animosity, were in turn killed, which served as a punishment for their heinous crimes.

However, no one kills Muslims today on account of religious resentment and prejudice, nor is the sword wielded against them due to their religion. Of course, worldly conflicts do occur amongst worldly people, but they are not our concern. So, in the present circumstances when no one takes up the sword to destroy Islam, it is immensely ignorant and contrary to the Quran to take up the sword under the cover of religion. If an individual appears in the world in the name of a bloodthirsty Mahdi or Messiah and incites people to fight the disbelievers, then it should be understood that such a person is a liar and an impostor who acts against the teachings of the Quran and follows a path which opposes it. I honestly say that those who subscribe to such beliefs do not follow the Quran. Rather, they worship the idol of ignorant custom and habit.

It is also ignorance and sheer folly on the part of the Christian clergy to unjustly go on clamouring that in Islam the Quran commands the spread of religion by dint of sword. In so doing, they incite and provoke the ignorant and simple-minded to further adopt false and absurd ideologies. These people have no knowledge of the Quran nor do they receive revelation from God so that it could be said that they attain knowledge of the Word of God from God Himself. As such, they unjustly continue to draw attention to an untrue concept.

God has bestowed upon me knowledge of the Quran and has granted me insight in understanding the Arabic language; without pride, I say that nobody in this land has been granted similar insight. Thus, I passionately affirm that the Quran does not teach in the least that religion be supported by the sword, nor does it instruct one to raise the sword against those who level criticisms. The Quran repeatedly teaches us to show patience in the face of injury caused by opponents. Therefore, one ought to be aware for certain that a Mahdi or Messiah who takes up the sword for religion will not at all be raised within Islam. A true religion penetrates the heart with arguments and not with the sword. In fact, aggression merely gives an opponent further pretext to object.

It is a great blessing of God Almighty that in order to rectify the erroneous ideas of such people, He has demonstrated the falsity of the physical descent of the Promised Messiah. By the grace of God, through my efforts, it has been proven that the Messiah, peace be upon him, did not ascend to the heavens with his physical body. In light of powerful argumentation and established events, people have no choice but to accept this. Instead, in accordance with the promise of God Almighty and the acceptance of his night-long supplications in which he prayed to be delivered, the Messiah, peace be upon him, was saved from death on the cross and the curse of crucifixion. Thereafter he migrated to India, where he engaged in religious debates with Buddhists. Eventually, he passed away in Kashmir and his sacred tomb is situated in Mohalla Khanyar. It is widely referred to as the tomb of the Prophet Prince.

When it has been proven that no one will descend from the heavens and instead the evidence is contrary to this, then the existence of a Mahdi who is to join forces with the Messiah and cause bloodshed must also be considered false. For, according to the rules of research and logic, if two premises are mutually dependent then the negation of one falsifies the other as well. Thus, one must accept that all these ideas are completely false, baseless, and absurd.

According to the Torah, one who is crucified becomes accursed. The word *la'nat* is common to both Hebrew and Arabic, and means to be completely estranged from God. Those who are accursed are divorced from Him as He is from them and they are His enemies as He is their enemy. God-forbid, no one who truly honours the Messiah could possibly disrespect this beloved, revered, and holy prophet in such a way. Moreover, events have further established that the Messiah, peace be upon him, was not crucified. Instead, he escaped the clutches of the disbelievers in his country and secretly travelled to India.

Therefore, the tales of these foolish Muslim clerics are false and their **savage hopes** are futile. They only give birth to pernicious ideas. If their beliefs were weighed against mine **in a court of law,** the extent to which they are entangled in vicious beliefs would become apparent. They are estranged not only from truth but also from peaceful practices.

In the end, I would like to conclude this treatise by saying that, whereas according to Christian doctrine the second coming of the Messiah has no political significance, the Muslim clerics of the current age erroneously believe that Jesus will descend from heaven and join with the Mahdi to wage a violent Jihad. This belief is not only false, but dangerous as well. However, the evidence I have recently unearthed regarding the migration of Jesus to India and his death in Kashmir is sufficient to fully cleanse the minds of all intelligent persons of these spurious ideas.

My research is not conjectural or cursory but very comprehensive. This investigation begins with the ointment known as *Marham-e-Isa*[1] or *Marham-e-Hawariyyin*[2] as it is otherwise known. It has been mentioned in more than a thousand books of medicine, and Zoroastrian, Jewish, Christian and Muslim physicians have alluded to it in their respective books. As I have spent a significant part of my life studying the science of medicine and have also discovered a large treasure trove of books, I have found evident proof that through the grace of God Almighty

---

1. The Ointment of Jesus [Publisher]
2. The Ointment of the Disciples [Publisher]

and the blessings of his own earnest supplications, Jesus, peace be upon him, was rescued from the cross. Thereafter, in his human dependence on the means of this world, he was administered the *Ointment of the Disciples,* by which were healed the wounds of his crucifixion—before migrating to India. He certainly did not die on the cross; rather, he merely experienced a kind of unconsciousness. Subsequently, in accordance with the will of God he spent three days in a cavernous tomb. Since he remained alive, like Jonah, he finally emerged therefrom. ☆

☆ **Note:** It is certain that Jesus, peace be upon him, did not die on the cross. He likened the three days he was to remain in his tomb to the case of the Prophet Jonah and his ordeal of the whale. Thus, he made clear to all discerning people that he entered the tomb alive in the likeness of the Prophet Jonah and remained alive therein. Otherwise, what resemblance can there exist between the dead and the living? The parallels expounded by the Prophets are never meaningless or in vain. The Gospel alludes to this elsewhere when it asks, 'Why do you look for the living among the dead?' The opinion of some of the disciples that Jesus had died on the cross was absolutely false. For his emerging from his tomb, showing his wounds to the disciples and likening his own situation to that of Prophet Jonah, all reject and oppose this notion.

Then, there is a difference of opinion among the disciples in this instance. The Gospel of Barnabas, which I have seen for myself, rejects the idea that Jesus, peace be upon him, died on the cross. Moreover, it is apparent from the Gospel that Barnabas himself was a respectable disciple and that the ascension of Jesus to the heavens was a spiritual event. Only that which comes from the heavens returns to them. The things of the earth remain herein. Both the Torah and the Quran testify to this. The Jews rejected the spiritual ascension of the Messiah because, in their view, he had died on the cross. Therefore, they were told that he ascended to heaven i.e. God Almighty saved Jesus and absolved him from being accursed, which is the result of death by hanging. How can

The second source for this research are the historical texts of various nations, which prove that Jesus, peace be upon him, definitely travelled through India, Tibet and Kashmir. Recently a Russian traveller has, through Buddhist texts, proven that Jesus, peace be upon him, came to this land. I have acquired and read his book and it supports the aforementioned view.

Finally, there is the tomb of the Prophet Prince, which is situated in Mohalla Khanyar, Srinagar. People refer to this as the burial place of Prince Yuz Asaf, the Prophet, while others say it is the tomb of *Isa Sahib,*[1] the Prophet, which further supports this thesis. Unlike other tombs, this one contains a window entrance, which is present even today. According to the belief of some Kashmiris this was fitted because the tomb contains some buried treasure. While it may well hide some jewels, in my understanding this window entrance was made because there is an inscription of singular importance within it.

These circumstances seem similar to a recent discovery in the village of Zilla Pirakoi which is located in a district on the northwest border of Nepal. A heavy chest was excavated from a mound there, which contained gems, jewellery, bone and ash. The chest was inscribed with the words 'the flowers of Gautama Buddha Shakyamuni'.

---

the testimony of a few disciples be accepted who were not present at the time of crucifixion and were, therefore, not eyewitnesses to the event? —Author

1. *Isa* is the Arabic form of the name Jesus and *Sahib* is used as a title of respect similar to English terms such as Mister, Honourable or Revered. [Publisher]

Furthermore, the word *nabi*,[1] so commonly used by thousands of Kashmiris with regard to the deceased one, is also an argument[☆] in favour of my claim. This is because the word *nabi* is common in both Hebrew and Arabic. It does not appear in any other language. It is an Islamic belief that after our Prophet, peace and blessings of Allah be upon him, no other prophet will appear. Therefore, this establishes that the Prophet under discussion is one from among the Hebrew Prophets. Further, when we ponder over the word *prince* the reality of the affair becomes more apparent.

Furthermore, the inhabitants of Kashmir unanimously agree that this Prophet whose grave is situated in Kashmir, lived six hundred years before our Prophet, peace and blessings of Allah be upon him. This is a clear reference to Jesus, peace be upon him. It is decisively established that this is the very same pious and pure Prophet, and the eternal prince of God Almighty's majestic throne whom the wretched and unfortunate Jews sought to crucify.

In short, this evidence is such that when all its arguments are considered collectively, they completely demolish the ideas of the iniquitous Muslim clerics, and the blessed edifice of peace and reconciliation shines brightly. This surely leads one to the

---

1. Prophet [Publisher]

☆ Another proof in support of my claim is that all the books that we have hitherto found regarding the life and teaching of Yuz Asaf, whose tomb resides in Srinagar, contain teachings which strongly resemble the moral teaching of the Gospel. In fact, certain phrases are exactly identical to those found in the Gospel. —Author

conclusion that neither did anyone ascend to heaven, nor would anyone come and fight alongside the Mahdi to cause mayhem. Rather, Jesus rests in peace in the lap of God's mercy in Kashmir.

Respected readers! Now I have presented all my principles, guidance and teachings before this distinguished government. The essence of my teachings is to live a life of reconciliation and modesty, and as subjects of this administration, i.e. the British government, be truly loyal and obedient without hypocrisy or worldly motive.

Lastly, I conclude with the prayer that God Almighty may continuously increase the prestige of our respected Queen, the Empress of India, may her prosperity endure; and may He grant us the ability to be sincere-heartedly loyal to her and become a peace loving people. *Ameen.*

Writer,
Humbly,
Mirza Ghulam Ahmad of Qadian
27 December 1898

Addendum to this Treatise

FOR THE ATTENTION OF
THE GOVERNMENT

After completing this treatise I received an English treatise
authored by the editor of *Isha'at-us-Sunnah,* Muhammad Husain
of Batala, published by the Victoria Press Lahore on 14 October
1898. I was greatly dismayed to see this treatise because of the
manner in which the author has very shamelessly lied about me
and about his belief regarding the advent of the Mahdi. He very
deceptively attempts to discredit me as a rebel in the eyes of the
eminent government. But, as the old adage has it—and how true
indeed—truth ultimately prevails. Therefore, I am confident that
this enlightened and perceptive government will swiftly discover
the truth of the matter.

The first untruth of Muhammad Husain mentioned in his
treatise, which he presents before the distinguished government
is that I am a danger to the government; that is to say, I harbour
rebellious aspirations at heart. But, I strongly state that if this were

true, I would prefer death to a life of disloyalty and treachery. With all due respect, I call on the esteemed government to investigate my state of affairs and teaching as minutely as possible. Further, they ought to question under oath those of my community members who are respected officials, Indian officers, chieftains, and other honourable and educated persons, and who number in the hundreds, as to the instructions I have given to them with reference to this benign government and the vigour with which I have advocated obedience to the state.

Moreover, the government should closely reflect on the testimony of Maulvi Muhammad Husain—which he himself wrote in *Isha'at-us-Sunnah* as a review of my book *Barahin-e-Ahmadiyyah* and which has been alluded to in this treatise as well—about the views of both my father, Mirza Ghulam Murtaza and myself, with regard to the British government. Moreover, the eminent government ought to carefully study those writings of mine which have been published over the past nineteen years in their support; in fact, investigate me from every angle. If, after this, the government considers my state of affairs to be questionable then it is my ardent desire that the government ought to give me the severest of punishments. However, if the reports of Muhammad Husain given to the government are found to be contrary to the facts, then as a loyal, well-wishing, and devoted citizen, I respectfully call on this benign government to admonish him for his false representations to the government, which contradict his own admission in his review of *Barahin-e-Ahmadiyyah* and which contradict the original view he held for twelve years without fail.

Now that he is my enemy, he accuses me of treachery, even though for nineteen years I have expressed my well wishes for this benign government through my pen and have conveyed my praise for the justice of this government in far-off countries, to such an extent that I can confidently say that no similar example can be found in the accomplishments of others. I am at a loss for words with which to humbly submit before the government how greatly the slanders fabricated by this individual have grieved and wounded me. How pitiful that he has intentionally and knowingly lied cruelly about me to the government and has sought to discredit all of my services. I have sound reasons and strong testimony in support of my claim. I am hopeful that because I belong to a loyal family that has proven its obedience to the government by offering its wealth and lives in its support, my painful request will be carefully heard by this beneficent administration and whoever is deemed a liar will be reprimanded.

The second thing which Muhammad Husain has written in this treatise is that I have published a revelation to the effect that the empire of this esteemed government will be destroyed in eight years. I can only respond to this calumny by calling on God to ruin the one who lies; I have never published any such revelation. All my books are present before the government. I respectfully call on them to inquire from this individual **in which book,** letter, or announcement **of mine have I published such a revelation?** I am hopeful that the honourable government will remain cautious of his deception in case he contrives a plan to reinforce his false statement and calls on some of his community and associates, who harbour deep animosity towards me on account of religious difference, to produce false testimony to the government. I have no relations and contact with this individual or those who share his ideas, so it cannot be said that I told them anything in person. It is in my books and announcements that I publish whatever I desire to articulate; therefore, my books and announcements are sufficient to inquire about my ideas and revelations. The honourable members of my community are also witnesses. Therefore, I respectfully request our revered government to interrogate Muhammad Husain about the deceitful informer who told him of this revelation. The former Deputy Commissioner of District Gurdaspur, Captain Douglas, has already noted during the case brought against me by Dr Martyn Clark that Muhammad Husain harbours enmity against me and this is why he does not refrain from lying about me.

The third matter which Muhammad Husain has written in this treatise is that I have falsely claimed to be the Promised Messiah. Here it is sufficient to write that just as the Prophets, peace be upon them, have had their prophethood proven over time, so too my God has proven my claim. Furthermore, the heavenly signs of God Almighty have given testimony in my support.

All that remains to be answered is why Muhammad Husain and his like-minded associates call me a liar and harbour such enmity against me? As I have already mentioned in this treatise, their enmity stems from the fact that my teaching goes against their aims and objectives; namely, against the belief that the Promised Messiah will descend from heaven and join forces with the Mahdi to war with the Christians.☆ They consider

---

☆ **Note:** Recently, in October 1898, Maulvi Muhammad Husain published a pamphlet in English so that the government would grant him some

the existence of the Mahdi necessary because in their view, the Promised Messiah cannot be a *Khalifah* as he does not hail from the Quraish. And Muhammad Husain has expressed his own belief as such in volume 12, page 380 of his magazine in commemoration of Sultan Abdul Hamid II ascending the throne of the Ottoman Empire. Therefore, such people have presented this very argument to establish the need for a Mahdi from the Quraish at the time of the second advent of the Messiah and have also mentioned many battles. I am certain that such creeds are extremely dangerous because a person who holds this belief always harbours thoughts of rebellion in their heart. I, however, oppose such beliefs. I do not believe in any such Messiah or Mahdi who will war with the disbelievers and distribute their wealth among the Muslim clerics and their people.

So it is for this reason that in their eyes I am a liar as my beliefs spell the ruin of all their hopes. I recognise that this teaching of mine has done untold damage to their aspirations, but this is no fault of mine. Rather, the fault lies in their own wrongdoings and misconceptions. **Muhammad Husain's statement in his treatise that he** does not believe in the Mahdi who is awaited by all of

---

land. He mentioned, contrary to his belief, that he rejects the advent of a Promised Mahdi, even though he has had me declared a heretic and antichrist on the basis of this belief. So he has shamelessly spoken a lie before the government. For he always preaches to his like-minded clerics that the Promised Mahdi will appear and fight the Christians and that Jesus, peace be upon him, will descend from the heavens to assist him in this. Yet Muhammad Husain says something entirely different to the government. I respectfully call on the honourable government to directly question the Muslim clerics regarding this matter so that the truth he has always sought to hide may be made known. —Author

his like-minded clerics and in whose support the Messiah will descend from the heavens as per their belief, is a completely hypocritical assertion, which he does not hold at heart.

Hundreds of Muslim clerics in the Punjab and India can testify that he believes in a bloodthirsty Mahdi, but he duplicitously hides the truth of his beliefs from the government. Like-minded clerics such as Maulvi Ahmadullah of Amritsar, Maulvi Rasheed Ahmad of Gangoh, Maulvi Abdul-Jabbar of Amritsar, Maulvi Muhammad Bashir of Bhopal, Maulavi Abdul-Haqq of Delhi, Maulvi Ibrahim Arah, Maulvi Abdul-Aziz of Ludhiana and particularly Maulvi Nazeer Husain of Delhi, who is a teacher of Muhammad Husain, ought to be asked under oath whether they believe that the Promised Mahdi will come and wage war and whether or not Muhammad Husain of Batala, the editor of *Isha'at-us-Sunnah,* is from among them and shares in their beliefs or not; also whether he believes that the *Khilafat* of this time can be occupied by anyone other than a person from the Quraish. These testimonies will reveal the extent of Muhammad Husain's hypocrisy before the government in the same way that the bones and innards of a corpse are revealed during their exhumation from a whitewashed and embellished grave.

I assure my wise and enlightened government that this individual holds the same belief about the Mahdi as do his like-minded friends, i.e. other Muslim clerics from the Punjab and the rest of India. The government can understand that it would be impossible for Muhammad Husain to hold a different view from the other Muslim clerics regarding such a widely accepted Islamic belief, and yet remain their friend and leader. A further proof of this is that in volume 12, page 380 of his *Isha'at-us-Sunnah,* he has clearly stated that '*Khilafat* is the due right only of the Quraish;

and no one from any other people can be a *Khalifah*.' It must then be pondered how he can suggest that the Messiah would be a king at the time of his second advent—because he is an Israelite and not from the Quraish. Furthermore, in the absence of the *Khalifah,* how can wars be waged? Therefore, all of the Muslim clerics have been forced to accept that at the time of the second advent of the Messiah, it is essential that there should be a *Khalifah* from the Quraish who should be a king of the time. If the coming of the Awaited Mahdi were to be denied, all of the beliefs of these people would be shattered. The descent of the Messiah from the heavens would also become futile because there would be no rightful *Khalifah* on earth in whose company the Messiah, peace be upon him, would fight the disbelievers.

It is for this reason that Muhammad Husain firmly believes that when the Messiah descends, the Promised Mahdi will surely be raised from among the Quraish; he will be the *Khalifah* of the age and the Promised Messiah will serve him along with those who pledge allegiance at his hand. For this reason, in their view the Hadith in *Sahih Bukhari,* i.e. [1] اِمَامُكُمْ مِنْكُمْ, alludes to the Promised Mahdi due to the words اِمَامٌ [*imam*] and مِنْكُمْ [*minkum*]; whereas, in my estimation, the word *imam* here refers to the Messiah who has been conferred spiritual authority. My view on this stands in stark contrast to that of Muhammad Husain and all his like-minded clerics who reside in the Punjab and throughout India. According to them the word *imam* in this Hadith alludes to the Awaited Mahdi who will be from the Quraish and who will wage war; and the Promised Messiah will serve him as

---

1. He will be your Imam from among you. [Publisher]

an adviser and counsellor, but the *Khalifah* of the time will be the Mahdi. In short, due to an incorrect understanding of the Hadith اَلْأَئِمَّةُ مِنْ قُرَيْشٍ [1] which is firmly grounded in their hearts, they believe that: *Khilafat* would ultimately return to the Quraish, the name of this *Khalifah* would be Muhammad Mahdi, he would descend from the Children of Fatimah and shed rivers of blood in the cause of religion.

If Muhammad Husain is simply asked: 'According to your belief, the Messiah would not be a *Khalifah* when he descends from the heavens as he would not be from the Quraish; who, then is the *Khalifah* who would wage war against the disbelievers? Furthermore, who is the Imam mentioned in the Hadith of *Bukhari*, اِمَامُكُمْ مِنْكُمْ.' These people will never say that the word *Imam* applies to the Promised Messiah, rather they will only respond by saying that the reference is to the Mahdi—namely, the one who will be from the Quraish. Thus, this question will expose their hypocrisy. It is worthy of note that Muhammad Husain does not consider the Hadith لَا مَهْدِيَّ اِلَّا عِيْسَى [2] to be valid and interprets the Hadith of *Bukhari* اِمَامُكُمْ مِنْكُمْ to refer to the *Khalifah* from the Quraish, and not to the Promised Messiah. Thus, it is established that he believes in the Mahdi and awaits his advent. How shameful, then, is the perjury of this man **who conveys one belief to the British government, but privately holds a contrary belief.**

If the respected authorities allow me to speak with him about this issue and if, during the course of discussion, his fellow clerics are also brought before us, it will become readily apparent that

---

1. The Imams will be from among the Quraish. [Publisher]
2. There is no Mahdi except Jesus. [Publisher]

this individual has thus far been deceiving the British government by stating that which is contrary to his deeply rooted belief.

When this question is posed, I have some of his writings in my possession that are sufficient to bring about his disgrace, which I prayed for to God Almighty regarding the one who is a liar in my announcement of 21 November 1898.

It is improper for anyone to utter **such brazen lies** before the government. Had he truly rejected the advent of the *Khalifah* from the Quraish—generally referred to as the Mahdi—and like me believed in a non-belligerent and non-violent Messiah, he too would perforce have had edicts declaring him to be a disbeliever as I have.

I assure the government that in this particular case, Muhammad Husain says one thing but believes another. In the company of his **like-minded** clerics he claims to hold the same belief as them. Yet when he writes something to please the government he simply states, '**I do not believe** that a Mahdi who wages war will appear.' However, if he does not believe in such a Mahdi, why does he claim to be the chief and advocate of those clerics that do? Justice in these matters now rests in the hands of the government. In my view, the government can easily ascertain the true beliefs of both of us if we are made to state our beliefs in their presence and in the presence of other Muslim clerics. At such a time, the whole truth regarding the one who is a hypocrite will be exposed. Thus,

I very respectfully request

that a judgement be made, especially since he has spoken such a blatant lie, how then can it be guaranteed **that he speaks the truth in other matters he brings before the government?** — Author

E N D

بِسْمِ اللّٰهِ الرَّحْمٰنِ الرَّحِيْمِ [1]

نَحْمَدُهٗ وَنُصَلِّیْ [2]

My prophecy of 21 November 1898 regarding the untruthful party, that is, the Arabic revelation [3] جَزَاءُ سَیِّئَۃٍ بِمِثْلِهَا *with reference to Muhammad Husain of Batala*

WAS FULFILLED

A Request to the Honourable Government to Peruse My Announcement

The following is a detailed account of the above mentioned matter. It involves two parties: on the one side, my community and I, and on the other, Maulvi Muhammad Husain and the followers of his community, such as, Muhammad Bakhsh Jafar Zatalli and Abul-Hasan of Tibet etc. On account of religious difference Muhammad Husain declared me an antichrist, a liar, an infidel and a disbeliever, and included in these edicts all the clerics

---

1. In the name of Allah, the Gracious, the Merciful. [Publisher]
2. We praise Him and invoke blessings upon His Noble Messenger[sa]. [Publisher]
3. The recompense of evil is a penalty in proportion thereto. [Publisher]

who follow him. Thus, as a result, they abuse me and hurl filthy invectives at me. After enduring these circumstances for quite some time, I finally issued an announcement for a prayer-duel on 21 November 1898. It included the following revealed words: جَزَاءُ سَيِّئَةٍ بِمِثْلِهَا. It prophesied that, of our two parties, the one which perpetrates grave injustices will face the same kind of humiliation which it sought for the other. So today, this prophecy has been fulfilled because Maulvi Muhammad Husain of Batala sought to humiliate me through his writings by declaring me as being opposed to a unanimously shared Muslim belief, and labelling me a heretic, a disbeliever and an antichrist. Further, he instigated the Muslims against me through such writings by stating that they ought to consider me a non-Muslim and one who does not follow the Sunnah of the Holy Prophet[sa] because my beliefs are not in accordance with theirs. But now the Muslims and their scholars have come to know after reading the **14 October 1898 edition** of his magazine, which was published in English as a means to acquire land from the British government that Muhammad Husain is himself opposed to their collective belief.

In this edition, he has categorically rejected the coming of a Promised Mahdi whose advent is awaited by all Muslims and who, in their view, will be born into the progeny of Hazrat Fatimah, be the *Khalifah* of the Muslims, the leader of their faith and who will fight religious wars against other denominations. Jesus, peace be upon him, will descend from heaven to help and assist him. Both will come with the same purpose and that is to spread religion with the sword. Now, Maulvi Muhammad Husain has categorically rejected the coming of such a Mahdi.

In doing so, he has not only denied the coming of the Mahdi, but has also been compelled to deny the coming of the Messiah who was supposed to descend from heaven to help this Mahdi, after which both were to fight against the enemies of Islam. Yet based on this exact same belief, Muhammad Husain declared me an antichrist and disbeliever. Hitherto, he had deceived the Muslims into thinking that he shared their beliefs. **But, now the veil has been lifted** that he, in fact, agrees with me and rejects the coming of such a Mahdi and Messiah. Hence, in accordance with the beliefs of the Muslims and their scholars he has become a heretic and antichrist. So today, the prophecy جَزَاءُ سَيِّئَةٍ بِمِثْلِهَا[1] has been fulfilled in his person, because this means that the unjust party will receive a punishment similar to the evil which it sought to inflict upon the other by action.

As for the allegation that I am a rebel of the British government, I am hopeful that by the grace of God Almighty, it will soon become clear to the government which of us is truly rebellious. He has recently written an inflammatory and dangerous article about me in his magazine *Isha'at-us-Sunnah,* number 3, volume 18, pages 98–100, with reference to the Sultan of Rome.[2] In summary, he writes that the Sultan of Rome ought to be considered a true *Khalifah* and accepted as a religious leader. One of his stated reasons in this article for declaring me a disbeliever is that I do not consider the Sultan of Rome to be a *Khalifah.* Although it is true that I do not consider the Sultan of Rome to be a *Khalifah,* in accordance with the conditions set by Islam,

1. The recompense of evil is a penalty in proportion thereto. [Publisher]
2. Abdul Hamid II [Publisher]

since he is not from the Quraish, whereas it is necessary for such *Khulafa* to be from the Quraish. However, this statement of mine is not against the teachings of Islam; in fact, it accords completely with the Hadith [1] اَلاَئِمَّةُ مِنْ قُرَيْشٍ. Alas, Muhammad Husain strayed from the teachings of Islam through this rebellious article. Previously, he himself had said that the Sultan is not the *Khalifah* of the Muslims or their religious leader. Now, in his enmity for me, the Sultan of Rome has become his *Khalifah* and religious leader, and in his passion he has paid scant regard to the British Empire and disclosed whatever was hidden in his heart by declaring the one who rejects the *Khilafat* of the Sultan of Rome to be a disbeliever. And all this passion was ignited because I praised the British Empire and said that they not only supported the Muslims in worldly terms, but also went further to support their faith. So, in order to incite rebellion he rejects the fact that any religious support has been afforded to us by the British and insists that the Sultan of Rome is the only patron of Islam. But this is manifest dishonesty. If this government is not our protector in religious matters, how then are we safe from the attacks of our enemies? Is there anyone who is unaware of our religious circumstances during the time of the Sikhs when the blood of Muslims would be shed for merely hearing the call to prayer? It was impossible for a Muslim cleric to convert a Hindu to Islam. Would Muhammad Husain care to answer where the Sultan of Rome was at that time? What help did he bestow upon us during this time of peril? So how can he be our religious leader and the true *Khalifah* of God? Ultimately, it was the British who

---

1. Imams will be from among the Quraish. [Publisher]

conferred favour upon us by removing our hurdles immediately upon their entry into the Punjab, after which our mosques were once again attended, our madrasas were opened, and we began to preach in public. Thousands of people from other religions began to enter Islam. So if I were to hold the belief, as does Muhammad Husain, that we submit to the government only due to political expediency, i.e. out of hypocrisy and that our hearts lie with the Sultan who is the *Khalifah* of Islam and our religious leader; and that to reject his being the *Khalifah* and to disobey him would be tantamount to disbelief, then undoubtedly I would be a hidden traitor to the British government and disobedient to God Almighty. It is strange that the government has not ascertained the truth of this matter and still lends an ear to such a hypocrite who says one thing to them and whispers something entirely different into the ears of Muslims. I respectfully request this eminent government to pay close attention to this individual's circumstances. He follows a course of hypocrisy and attributes to me the rebellious ideas that he himself entertains.

Finally, it is important to write that this individual has hurled vile abuse at me and incited Muhammad Bakhsh Jafar Zatalli to do the same. He has sought to humiliate me by fabricating all sorts of lies. So I call on God who knows the secrets of the heart and by whose hand justice is dispensed, that this individual also suffer the same disgrace that he sought to bring upon me through his false accusations, to the extent that he even misstated the facts, so as to portray me as a traitor to this benign government. I do not desire for him that he suffer any other humiliation except for that which has been described in the words [1] جَزَآءُ سَيِّئَةٍ بِمِثْلِهَا and, as the aggrieved party, it is my desire that if I am not guilty of the allegations made against me then may he be humiliated in the manner that he has sought to disgrace me.

I am certain that this government is most tolerant and forgiving insofar as possible, but if I am a rebel as Muhammad Husain claims, or if he himself holds rebellious ideas as I have come to know, then it is obligatory on the government to fully investigate this matter and punish appropriately the true culprit from among the two of us so that such evil does not take root in the country. The easiest course to maintain peace is to question renowned Muslim clerics of the Punjab and the rest of India regarding the beliefs of the man whom they have taken as their leader and advocate. Does he express the same beliefs to the government as he does to them? For it is essential that he hold the same belief as the clerics that he represents and for whom he advocates.

In the end, I also wish to draw the attention of the government to the fact that in his *Isha'at-us-Sunnah,* volume 18, number 3, page 95, Muhammad Husain has incited his followers by stating that I am **deserving of death.** So, as a prominent leader who has issued an edict☆ against me, on account of the justice

---

1. The recompense of evil is a penalty in proportion thereto. (*Surah Yunus,* 10:28) [Publisher]

☆ **Note:** When Muhammad Husain issued this edict of death, he falsely accused me of blaspheming against Jesus, peace be upon him, and thus stated that I deserve to be put to death. But, this is a blatant lie on the part of Muhammad Husain. I claim to be the Promised Messiah and say that I bear a resemblance to Jesus, peace be upon him. Thus, everyone can understand that if I were, God-forbid, to insult Jesus, peace be upon

of this distinguished government, I am hopeful that any legal action that such an individual deserves be allowed to take its course without hindrance in order to ensure that his followers do not plan my murder, seeking the reward of God. The end.

Writer,
Humbly,
Mirza Ghulam Ahmad of Qadian
27 December 1898

him, why would I state that I resemble him? For this would be to under-mine my own self. —Author

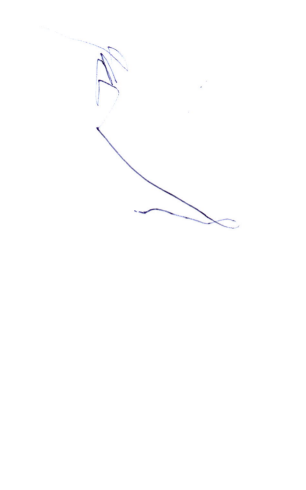